Chicago Clarity

Rich Hebron

Chicago Clarity

Rich Hebron

Books by Rich Hebron

Homeless but Human
Primary Ponderings

Nuance & Notes Series

Chicago Clarity
Paris Beauty
New York Energy
Los Angeles Dreams
Miami Magic
Milwaukee Sensibility
Mexico City Merriness
London Happening

Written by Rich Hebron
Illustrated by Kenneth Ferguson

Milly Moves to the Farm
The Boy and the Rocketship

Rich Edition Classics

The Great Gatsby

Rich Hebron is an American author. He has lived half his life in Chicago and the other half on a farm in rural Wisconsin. He fuses these backgrounds together to draw inspiration and live a meaningful life in a world accelerated by the internet and digital technology. He hosts the Rich Conversations Podcast where he explores self-development and talks with friends in art and science fields.

Connect with Rich: @richhebron

For those who want to live with clarity

Author's Note

My first near-death experience happened on the farm. An oil line blew on the tractor and became engulfed in flames. I jumped from it. My second near-death experience occurred four years afterwards. This time, three men pointed Uzi guns at my face, threatening to shoot me. Fortunately, it was just another reminder that life will end—all our lives. So how do we want ours to be?

After initially going fast, with the adrenaline from the encounter lasting months, I decided to stop. The difference between speed and velocity is that velocity is speed in a direction. Anyone can go fast—especially in circles. But it takes skill and something deeper to channel energy with purpose. Refining purpose requires restarting at the beginning. Be open and see what's happening. Pursue curiosity and, above all, patience.

My curiosity led me to hotel lobbies. I spent time visiting different ones in downtown Chicago and just sat, observed, and wrote notes, often sipping espresso or red wine. An appreciation for details developed. Gratitude followed. Every thing was there for a reason. Nothing was a coincidence. The creators of the spaces aimed to evoke particular emotions and feelings in people. They staged a vibe.

I learned that design affects our mind and influences our culture. The whole of something is the result of individual things. From a pencil to a house. From a shoe to our cities. From a light fixture to our lives. The story of our life is the result of every individual decision we make. The universe is the result of every individual atom.

Beauty is the result of those small, individual components. Love is understanding those small, individual components.

My passion and appreciation for detail expanded from hotel lobbies to virtually everything in life and in people. But something I especially had fun with was observing the designs on building facades. My favorites were those resembling nature. They possessed the character I aspire to be: dynamic, flexible, playful, and fruitful. Things that are alive are adaptable. Things that are dead are stiff, rigid, and brittle. Since human beings are part of nature, the same is true for people and their ideas and perspectives.

I encourage you to reflect on the follow questions:

- *Are current environments failing to design nuance?*
- *If design affects culture, what are the ramifications of prioritizing cheap and fast?*
- *Is a society that ignores patience a healthy one?*
- *If individuality is abandoned, is Love too?*

This is a series called *Nuance & Notes*.
This is a book of nuance of Chicago with notes from my mind and observations in the world.

There's a saying in Chicago that "Chicago's where you go to get great." It is that—a great American city. It's the crown jewel of the Midwest. The mix of the city's blue collar work ethic and gorgeous architecture creates a culture of pride. Big things happen here. It's a city that doesn't need to say anything, which results in a coolness that permeates the people and the streets. With its fresh lake and intentional emphasis on nature, one has the ability to breathe, think, and be in peace.

Shot on iPhone 13 Mini

Start with
gratitude and patience

Fear leads to less thought

Failure is interpretation
if we understand the journey we're on

Rich Hebron

Wellness is important
Let's prioritize it

Redesign what needs updating
Increase the usefulness from before

An ecosystem thrives
when each part is healthy

We'll feel better
reducing what we no longer need

Let's discover what we like
rather than what everyone else likes

We all have value to share
with the world
Go within and discover it

Align our mind with nature
We'll be well

Decide what we're doing
Decide what we're not doing

We're grateful for our friends
Our friends bring us joy
We love our friends

First observe what we have
Start there

We're grateful for the opportunity
We'll learn and grow

Organizing our life can be fun

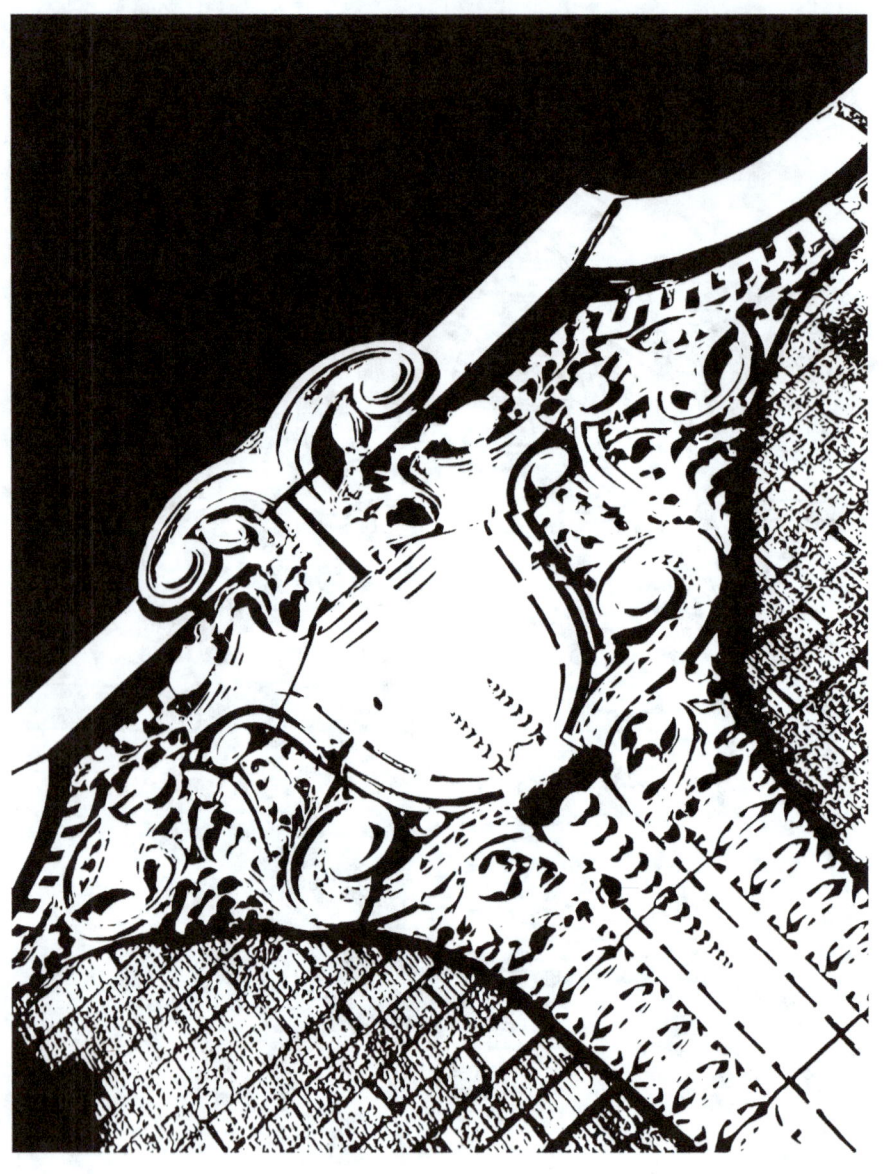

Today is excellent

Don't overthink this

Rich Hebron

Have a place for every thing
Our mind will appreciate it
Clarity follows

If we need a machine to exercise
If we need a gym to exercise
We'd be a weak human being

Let's help connect people together

What's sexier than a night's great sleep?

With material possessions
Do we use this?
How specifically would we use this?
Act on our answers

Unsubscribe from what we don't use

Where do we exert our energy?
Be conscious

Don't do what everyone does
Do what we do

Rich Hebron

Begin with one foot forward
Take another foot forward

It's about us
together

Prescribe flowers to reduce anger

Why do we fear?
Let's fear less

Rich Hebron

Create motions in the morning
that we're energized to perform

Are we here?
Why are we over there?
Be here now

Nature always returns to calmness
Let's also

Do we love all?
If not,
we're only thinking of our self
Do better

Those with much energy
distribute
Those with little energy
distribute

Electrify our communities

Rich Hebron

It's a joy to listen to others
We can learn

Why is the garden gated?
Let's open it together

Rich Hebron

Our potential can be unlocked with fun

Plant plants
Breathe

Plants help clear the space we're in

Let's put forth effort here

Work with others
More will be completed

Make wellness normal

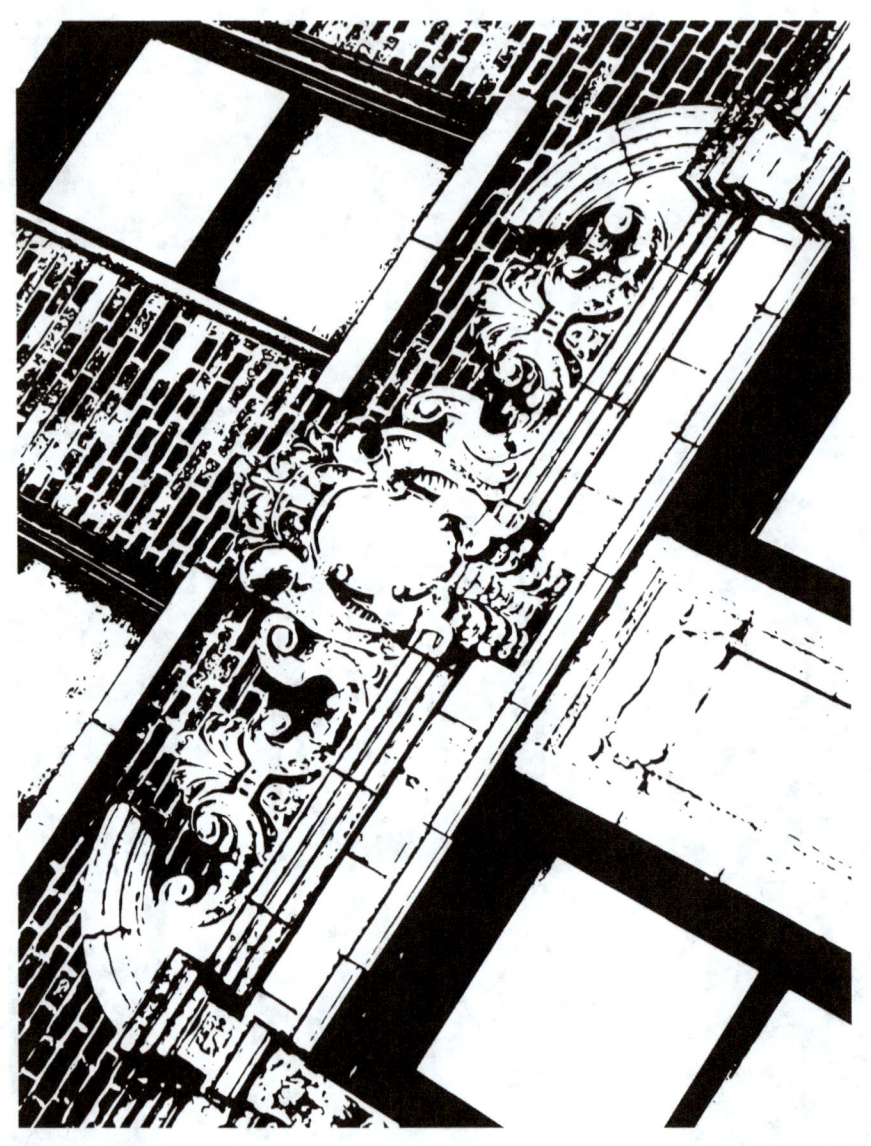

Energy isn't in a book
Energy is in us
Energy is in the world

What's healthier
rising when we're energized
or rising when we're told?

Decide how we'll use the internet
Use it only that way
No other

Evergreen is more lasting

Every thing is by design
So what is this for?

Sit down
Breathe

Rich Hebron

We have so much energy right now

To feel clearer
Simplify our life

Rich Hebron

We can be grateful
now and always

Theory is limited
Test in real life

Rich Hebron

Each moment we decide
whether we live
in an artificial or natural world

Do we inspire our self?
Take actions to ensure it

The more clear we are
the stronger we'll be

Generosity is magic

Rich Hebron

Decide what to care about
Care about it

Imagine living in Fear
Let's not live like that
That's not us

Let's help others
Let's be generous to more

Each moment is a moment
to express our gratitude

Let's design an ecosystem that thrives
It'll be vibrant and beautiful

Be energized for today

Rich Hebron

Let's not torment our self
through making bad decisions

Be patient with our future
Be clear and take steps

We can think of many things
we appreciate

It feels good to be with people
who share values with us
Understand that and zoom out

Rich Hebron

More questions
Less opinions

There's no reward
for knowing the news
There's punishment though

Rich Hebron

Be open to people
Have conversations

We can exercise any where

We can create whatever we want
So what future do we want?

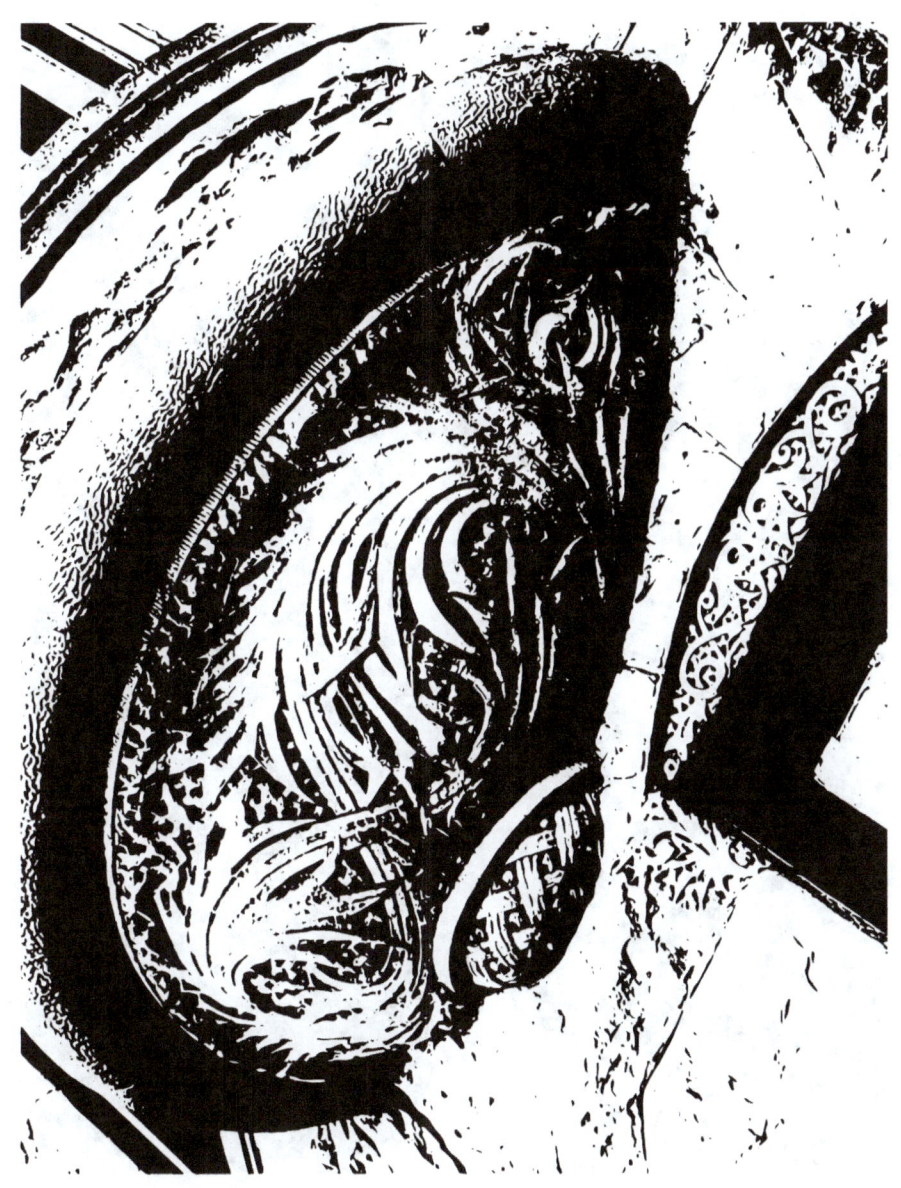

The more we do
the more we'll do more

Rich Hebron

Clarity follows simplicity

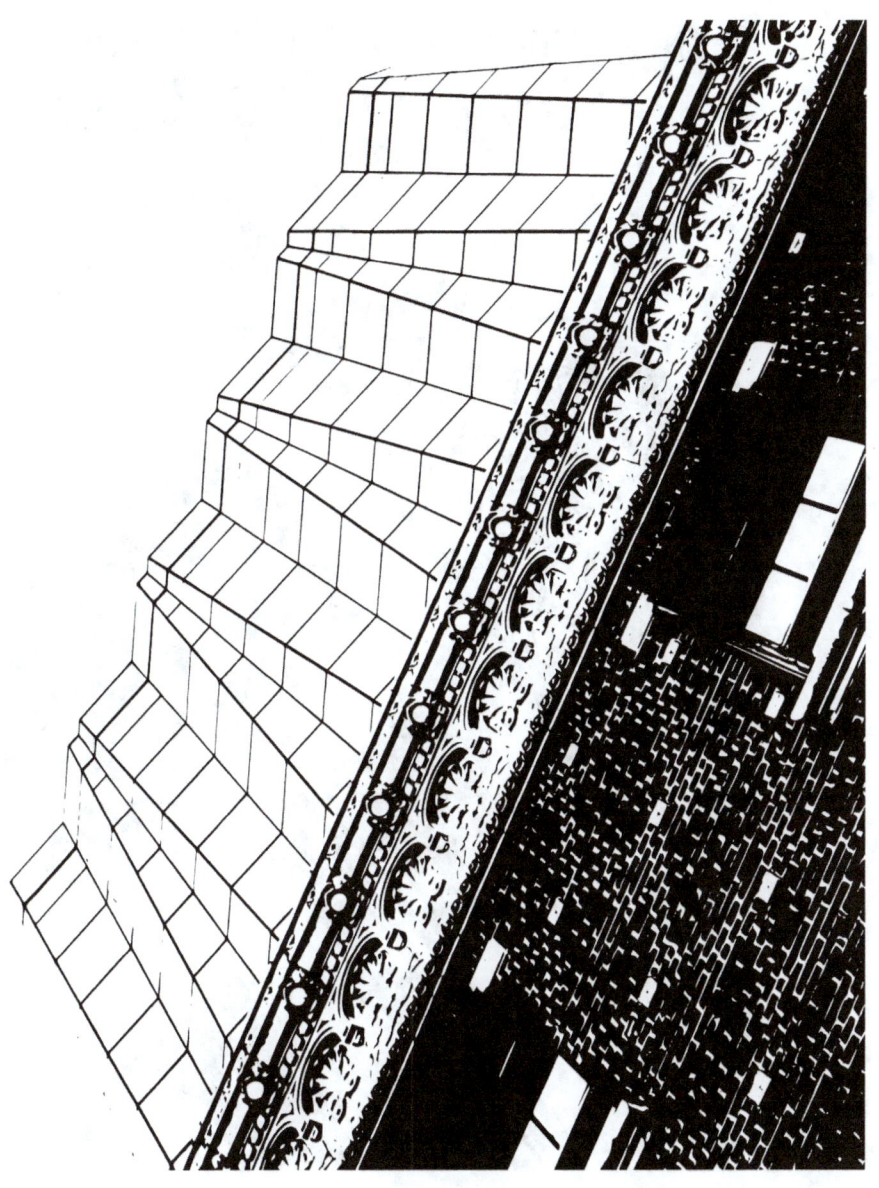

Don't grow tired
Grow energized

Rich Hebron

Monitor our thoughts
Our life will reflect them

Be clear not clever

Success can be full of wonder
Enjoy
We practiced patience

Let's keep gratitude on our mind
It's helpful

Rich Hebron

How is this presented?
We choose based on it

The more people
the more opportunity

Let's be grateful for the ability of vision

The world is not black and white
The world is gray
Navigate it

Rings are informative
whether on a tree or hand

Nature is flowing
Flow with it

Rich Hebron

What if it's easy?
Who told us it's hard?

There's an abundance
when we're our best
Share our energy with others

Celebrate with humility
It'll inspire rather than provoke envy

Smile with the sun

When we have lemons,
we can choose what to do with them

Things are happening
Do we see them?

Rich Hebron

We have no enemies
Time would be closest
But if we align with nature
our time will be enough

Sometimes a smile is most effective

Understand basic concepts of physics
Apply them to our life

Encouragement inspires no limits
Fear discourages falling

Rich Hebron

Let's clear our mind,
so we can be here now

Discipline creates freedom
Design boundaries that work for us
and our vision

Learn learn learn
Discomfort discomfort discomfort

Discipline is our friend
Organization is our friend also

A simple life is a beautiful life

We each play a role
Play it well
Each role is vital

We don't have to wait
We can empower our self now and here

What are others wearing?
What are we wearing?
We communicate through our choices

Know what provokes Fear inside us
We'll know the direction to follow

We're all here at the same time
Understand and enjoy that
We share time

Lighten the burden for others
by sharing the gifts we have

Put thought into our actions
Let them be natural

People remember
how we make them feel
not what we say

Does each day have a certain vibe?
Is it caused by the movement of people?

When did we last sing our loudest?

It's not what music we want to play
it's what energy the crowd wants to feel

We can see clearer
if we take a step back

Perfect is nonexistent for all
But we can live perfect for us

Review our actions
Interpret the results
Identify how to proceed forward

What are we most consistent with?
What does that signal to us?

Things are how they are
because of imagination
or lack of imagination

We know it'll rain
from dark clouds in the sky
Nature is simple

When stuck
think with simplicity

We don't live
in an independent world
We're a part
of a connected world

Don't wait for another to rescue us
We have the power within us
to figure this out

Our life will be fantastic
with the balance of
silence, laughter, and music

Be grateful for the energy
our past selves put into experiences
It got us here

Less words the better

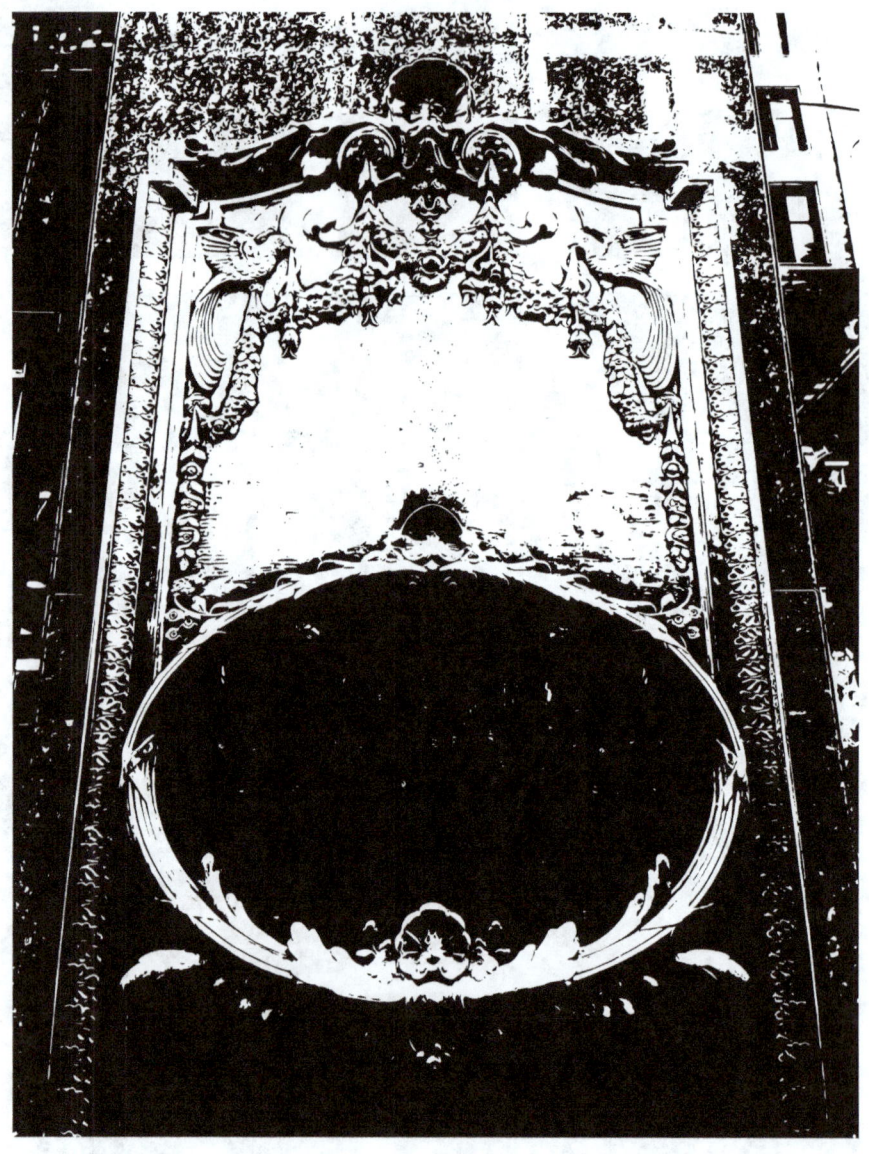

Don't miss the nuance of the moment
It's kind and generous to us

Some see the bark of a tree
Some see the forest
Collaboration is best

If life is a dream,
what will it be?

Our actions accumulate
toward our dreams

A Thought on Cities

Our cities are our greatest invention. They're the engines of civilization. Cities are the hubs that bring people, ideas, and opportunities together. They generate energy and inspire the pursuit of dreams and a better life.

I feel humans are meant to be isolated in nature or surrounded by other humans. Fusing the two maximizes energy and accelerates regenerative processes. This is why I shuffle between living on a farm in rural America and traveling to big international cities.

Having lived in Chicago for over 15 years, I am an enthusiastic advocate for urban living. I believe that the healthier the city, the more dynamic the society and culture. I'm passionate about exploring and analyzing the facets of each city. I believe in competition and that our cities should be constantly learning, adapting, evolving, and growing to serve and increase the quality of life for its residents. I love observing and comparing cities, noting their strengths and weaknesses, the effects of local geography, the movements and flows, and how every small matter contributes to the larger matter.

Cities are where big things happen. I believed this as a little kid growing up on a farm and I know it now as an adult who has experienced their impact.

I'm proud to combine notes that can help realize individual human potential with artwork that demonstrates the beauty collaboration can produce.

Rich leads weekly self-reflection sessions
to help people gain more clarity

Join in on the Rich Conversations Podcast
or visit the Rich Hebron YouTube channel

Connect with Rich: @richhebron

Notes

Notes

Notes

Notes